Real Life Financial Planning

An Easy to Understand System to Organize Your Financial Plan and Prioritize Financial Decisions

Todd D. Bramson, CFP

Published by Aspatore, Inc.

For corrections, company/title updates, comments or any other inquiries, please e-mail info@aspatore.com.

First Printing, 2004

10 9 8 7 6 5 4 3 2 1

ISBN 1-59622-017-1 Library of Congress Control Number: 2004107996

Material in this book is for educational purposes only. This book is sold with the understanding that neither any of the authors or the publisher is engaged in rendering medical, legal, accounting, investment, or any other professional service. For legal advice, please consult your personal lawyer. This book is printed on acid free paper.

The views expressed by the individuals in this book do not necessarily reflect the views shared by the companies they are employed by (or the companies mentioned in this book).

About ASPATORE BOOKS –
Publishers of C-Level Business Intelligence

www.Aspatore.com

Aspatore Books is the largest and most exclusive publisher of C-Level executives (CEO, CFO, CTO, CMO, Partner) from the world's most respected companies and law firms. Aspatore annually publishes a select group of C-Level executives from the Global 1,000, top 250 law firms (Partners & Chairs), and other leading companies of all sizes. C-Level Business Intelligence ™, as conceptualized and developed by Aspatore Books, provides professionals of all levels with proven business intelligence from industry insiders – direct and unfiltered insight from those who know it best – as opposed to third-party accounts offered by unknown authors and analysts. Aspatore Books is committed to publishing an innovative line of business and legal books, those which lay forth principles and offer insights that when employed, can have a direct financial impact on the reader's business objectives, whatever they may be. In essence, Aspatore publishes critical tools – need-to-read as opposed to nice-to-read books – for all business professionals.

Dedication

This book is dedicated to my immediate family: My parents, David and Fran, my wife and best friend Jerilyn, my children Ali and David, and my sister Julie. Also, to all relatives, in laws and extended family who enrich our personal life. Without the love, support and guidance of all of these people, I wouldn't have learned the most important lesson of life…..."When all is said and done, it is the quality and depth of relationships and experiences that are the essence of life…not the accumulation of material possessions."

Thank You

I extend a special thank you to…..

…my clients who have trusted me with their financial decisions

…my staff, partners, and business associates who make work a pleasure.

…Leslie Millikan for listening, offering insight and constructive ideas as my business "coach"

…all of those special people who I have learned from, **especially** Dick and Kathy Anderson, Ed Deutschlander, John Gadow, Joel Huth, Dick Koob, Bob Logas, Shaun McDuffee, Paul Mershon, Phil Richards, Scott Richards, Art Sanger, Herb Schmiedel, Mark Schweiger, Dave Smrecek, Nick Stevens, Dave Vasos, Diane Yohn, Pete and Jody Witte and Andy, Brad, Dan, Jeff, Pete, Scott.

Lastly, a special thank you to Mishelle Shepard who kept encouraging and helping me throughout the process of writing this book. This would still be handwritten ideas on a yellow scratch pad if it wasn't for you.

Real Life Financial Planning

C<small>ONTENTS</small>

Foreword

I have gained wisdom, strength of character, integrity, empathy, and the value of giving by my parents' example. Unfortunately, my father passed away very suddenly at the age of 45, when I was just 16. It was three weeks from the day he discovered a few black and blue marks on his arms to the day he died of acute leukemia. In this short time, we never had a chance to talk about the future, although I feel his guidance through my conscience and in the wisdom of others, including my mother.

It is interesting how the experiences of childhood, both good and bad, mold the path we follow as adults. My dad did not have much life insurance, or any established relationships with trusted advisors. When he died, my mother was lost financially. She was given very poor financial advice and the small amount of life insurance she had was lost in an unsuitable and inappropriate investment. My family's misfortune defined my passion. It was through this unfortunate situation that I became empowered. My mission has remained intact for over 25 years as I decided this would never happen to my family or anyone who entrusted me with their important financial decisions.

Due to our significant financial crisis I became eligible for an Evans Scholarship. In the early 1930's, Chick Evans became a nationally ranked golfer and started a college scholarship program with his earnings instead of turning pro. This scholarship has now grown to the largest privately funded scholarship in the country. There are over 820 students currently benefiting from it as well as over 8,000 alumni. His vision and generosity has been an inspiration to me.

With that in mind, this book is my benevolence. I am now in the fortunate position of being able to give back. Some of the proceeds from this book will be given to charity, including the Evans Scholars

Foundation, Breakfast Optimist Foundation, MDRT Foundation, Madison Community Foundation, St. James Lutheran Church, Leukemia Society, and many others. I am interested in "partnering" with other charities to help in their fund-raising efforts and I encourage you to contact me to discuss those possibilities.

I'd like to share a proverb containing some valuable wisdom and insight:

He (or She!) who knows, and knows he knows, is wise;
Follow him.
He who knows, but knows not that he knows, is asleep;
Awaken him.
He who knows not, and knows he does not know, is simple;
Teach him.
He who knows not, but does not know that he knows not, is dangerous;
Avoid him.

I believe it's our mission in life to listen to and learn from, or **follow** those who fall into the first category. But it is also our mission to take our unique gifts and make them available to those who are asleep or simple by **awakening** and **teaching** them. Also, time is too precious to spend with those who are dangerous. **Avoid** and minimize the amount of time you spend with people who fall into this category, and your enjoyment of life will multiply. We all have unique gifts and abilities and to the extent that our lives overlap and intertwine, we can all grow together carrying out our unique visions.

It is my hope that this book will educate and help you to achieve all of your personal and financial goals.

Todd D. Bramson
June, 2004
Madison, WI

1

The Basic Questions

Why the title Real Life Financial Planning?

I have spent over twenty years working directly with individuals on their financial plans and financial planning questions. There is so much information "out there," but sometimes not much wisdom. Hopefully this book summarizes the wisdom I have learned and shared with my clients in individual meetings throughout the years. *Real Life Financial Planning* is simply a practical method of understanding, organizing and prioritizing financial decisions.

Most financial planning publications and financial plans themselves assume everyone lives a long, healthy life and saves a good portion of their income in quality investments that always do well. This book addresses all of the issues that happen in real life, and I hope you take the time to read this and work with a trained professional to develop and implement a financial plan that meets *your* goals and objectives.

Why is there is an ever-increasing number of financial planning books on the market today?

Because there is an ever-increasing need to get educated.

- Few parents openly discuss financial matters with their children while they're growing up.
- Personal financial planning is rarely a subject taught in school.
- Many young people today begin their professional life already *in the red* when you consider the average student who takes out a college student loan graduates with over $20,000 in debt.
- We live high pressure, busy lifestyles that don't allow much free time to try and learn about all of the options that we have.

These unfortunate facts mean there are far too many people today who are ill-equipped to deal with the practical and fundamental necessities of planning for a secure and independent financial life.

Times have changed. Today, more than ever, your financial future needs you. Long gone are the days when you could rely on your company to pay back decades of loyal service with a comfortable pension plan. Even the government can't assure you of a reasonable retirement after a lifetime of social security contributions. Not to mention the fact that financial issues have become increasingly complex and we are continually inundated with confusing financial information.

These facts aren't meant to stress you out, but to wake you up to the financial reality of America today. It's not simply a matter of whether you will be able to retire rich, but whether you will simply be able to sustain your current lifestyle for the rest of your life.

Don't wait another day. This book is meant to give you an introduction into the often intimidating world of financial planning. You will taste some of the tempting varieties of investments. You will sample from the sea of insurance options. You will learn the lingo and get advice on where to go to next, whether you intend to go the road alone or get some help along the way. Best of all, you will climb the pyramid of financial success.

Financial success isn't, as most people might suspect, the ability to make one or two decisions that turn a buck into a million. Rather, financial success is the result of many, many small but sound decisions that, when compounded, add up to substantial financial security.

You are in complete control. Or at least you should be. When it comes to spending and saving, investing and paying taxes, many may offer good advice, but you're the only one who can do anything about it. Maybe you're a chronic shopper. Maybe you're unsure of your investment options and how to prioritize them. Maybe you don't have a clue where your paycheck goes each month. In any case, if you're reading this book you already understand the importance of getting your future under control, and that's the crucial first step to financial freedom.

Who Needs a Financial Planner?

Financial independence and the accumulation of wealth are no accident. Granted it's not possible to plan for every single event in life, but even tragedy can feel more manageable when you are financially prepared for it. *If you're like many people, you probably spend more time planning for a vacation than for your entire financial future!* Whether it's preparing for the future, securing yourself and your family against tragedy or planning for the good times, your money deserves your undivided attention.

Car accidents, marriage, divorce, kids, corporate downsizing, death, retirement, for better or worse, are the realities of life. Planning for any circumstance, both happy and sad, may seem like a burden right now, but the right planning will rescue you when (not if!) unforeseen circumstances arise. Sometimes, solid planning can even turn otherwise bad fortune into good—maybe that downsizing could lead to a better job, or the divorce to a healthier situation, or the pregnancy may provide the chance to take more time off to spend with your family than you thought you could.

The truth is, we all need to plan for our financial futures. So the question is not whether to plan, but how to go about making a plan, and whether we need a professional to help. The *information age* has intensified the field of financial planning. It is interesting to consider that twenty years ago financial news may have made top headlines two or three times throughout the year when the stock market would do particularly poorly or well, or if there was some other major economic news. Today, however, we have news programs dedicated to nothing else 24-7, and the number of financial headlines in the daily papers can be overwhelming. Still, there is a big difference between information and wisdom, and that's where the insight of a trusted professional can help.

Several situations which may call for a financial planner's expertise are:

- *You are a professional without much spare time.* If you're working for a good company they may provide the groundwork for investing wisely for the long term, but even the best can't take into consideration the special circumstances of each individual or family. In this case a financial planner can save you a bit of your most precious commodity—time.

- *You are easily bored or overwhelmed by financial questions.* If, for example, preparing a budget is such a nuisance that you can't even imagine having to sort through anything more complex, like insurance options, trends in mutual funds or the stock market, then hiring a financial planner may be money well spent for greater peace of mind.

- *You are considering a complicated set of employee benefits in combination with personally owned insurance and investments.* You certainly don't want a new employer (or an existing employer who has changed their benefit structure) to conflict or overlap with your current investments. Such gaps or possible duplications should be examined thoroughly.

- *You are recently divorced or have lost a spouse who had previously been the one handling financial affairs for the household.* As if dealing with the trauma of divorce or death is not enough, being thrust into unknown financial waters without a trusted advisor can make you feel you're trying to stay afloat with bricks chained to your ankles.

- *You have recently graduated from high school or college and are suddenly expected to become financially independent.* The saying "an ounce of prevention beats a pound of cure" is an important one in the world of financial planning. Seemingly insurmountable debt plagues the future of many young people. Learning to budget properly, to choose from insurance options and to make wise investments are necessary life skills. Getting professional advice now beats paying for costly mistakes later.

- *You are self employed.* In this case, you most likely have to "wear many hats" as an entrepreneur. You are in manufacturing, sales, accounting, customer servicing, and probably don't have time to investigate or be aware of the many planning options available to you for you and your employees. A financial planner can help you sort through the many issues facing you.

As much as some of us would like to leave it all up to a professional, it's crucial that you understand the basics. A financial advisor is someone there to educate and advise you and assist you in taking action to implement a plan, but ultimately the final decisions are yours. A good financial planner will educate you as to the options you face, acting as a teacher, so that you understand all of the relevant issues. Then you can work together to implement a plan, and monitor it over the years. A successful financial plan is an ongoing process that stays up to date with your situation.

The topic doesn't matter....whether it's religion, politics, stocks, insurance, sales loads or how to finance your house, just to name a few. There are always many individual considerations, and the correct solution depends on a variety of factors. I get leery of advice that suggests you should "always" do this or "never" do that. I believe life is far more gray than it is black and white.

I am not the first to say this, and I certainly won't be the last: *"It is crucial to trust your own judgment and instincts before taking action, no matter how good someone makes their argument."* The best way to gain confidence in your own better judgment is to educate yourself on the topic at hand.

With that in mind, in this book, you'll find answers to the most important financial questions facing everyone:

- How much money should I have in emergency reserves?
- In which order should I go about paying off my debts?
- Which is the right kind of insurance for me & how much do I need?
- What are the most common financial mistakes people make?

If you don't know the answers yet, don't worry; just keep reading, because you're about to find out.

2

Where Do I Start?

Your Net Worth Statement

The starting point of any financial plan is to figure out your current net worth. This is a snapshot of what you are worth at an exact point in time. In order to determine your net worth you simply add up all of your assets and subtract all of your liabilities (debts). Sometimes, when you are just starting out, the net worth is actually a negative number because the liabilities exceed the assets.

In order to measure your financial progress it is important to know your net worth. Many people measure their financial progress by how much money they have in the bank. In reality, as the value of your assets go up, such as a house, business or investments, and as you pay debts down, your net worth may be increasing more dramatically than you think. The most important way to measure financial progress is to calculate your net worth regularly.

Don't panic! Here's where we have to get just a bit technical. Before you shake your head and think; "*Whoa, this looks way too involved for me,*" just try taking it one step at a time, following the chart and example below. After you learn how to do it once, it'll be just like riding a bike.

In simple terms, what would you be worth if you sold everything you owned and turned it into cash, then paid off all your debts? If this is the first time you're preparing a net worth statement, it's also a good idea to try and estimate what you think your net worth has been over the last few years. Hopefully you will be pleasantly surprised at the progress you've made.

Refer to the simple example of a net worth statement on page 23.

There are several categories within the net worth statement.

Fixed assets is the first category. Fixed assets are those assets that do not have a risk of a loss of principal. These would include the most conservative assets you have money in. A few examples would be checking and savings accounts, money market funds, certificates of deposit, T-bills, EE savings bonds and whole life insurance cash values. These would be assets that you have access to in an emergency, they are available now and so are considered liquid.

Variable assets include most other financial assets. Examples include stocks, bonds, mutual funds, retirement plans or any investment where the principal can fluctuate.

Your personal and other assets would include tangible assets such as your house, personal or business property, and vehicles. Other tangible assets such as a stereo, computer, camera, etc. would also be included here.

Don't get too bogged down trying to establish a value for every piece of personal property. You may already have that information available from your homeowner's or renter's insurance policies, but if not, a rough estimate will work just fine. The main reason for gathering this information is to have an estimate so that you can monitor trends. This

Fixed Assets:
        Savings Account: $5,000
        Checking Account: $3,000
        Certificate of Deposit $2,000
        Total Fixed Assets: **$10,000**

Variable Assets:
        IRA: $3,000
        Mutual Funds: $5,000
        Individual Stocks: $2,000
        Variable Life Cash Value: $4,000
        401k balance: $20,000
        Total Variable Assets: **$34,000**

Personal and Other Assets:
        Home: $200,000
        Vehicle: $20,000
        Personal Property $20,000
        Total Personal & Other: **$240,000**
Total Assets: **$284,000**

Liabilities:
        Mortgage: $160,000
        Home Equity Line of Credit $5,000
        Vehicle Loan: $10,000
        Credit Cards: $2,000
        Total Liabilities: **$177,000**
Net Worth: Assets minus Liabilities$107,000

way, when you are reviewing your net worth after some time, you will be able to track how this category has changed or to account for some of the money you spent.

Tip: Use a video camera to film each room in your house, including closets and the garage. In the event of a loss, it will be much easier to remember for insurance company's reporting purposes.

For your liabilities, list the amount that you owe if you could pay off the amount today, not the total of the payments over time, which would include interest. Subtract your total liabilities from your assets to arrive at your net worth. If you're like many people, this can be a sobering experience. Don't forget to include all loans, like mortgages, auto loans, credit cards, student loans, personal debts and consumer debt.

Don't feel too upset if you learn your net worth is negative. For many people in the first stages of financial planning, it is the seemingly unmanageable debt that whips their spending habits into shape and pushes them to start planning for the future. It is also not unusual for recent graduates or those who have just finished some form of job training or other education to have a negative net worth because of student loans. However, remember that education is not a needless expense and should be consider as an investment in your financial future.

If you fit into the negative net worth category your first financial goal is to get your new worth back to zero. For you, it is especially important to establish a financial plan and get control of your financial life as soon as possible. But, instead of dreading the process, have some fun with it. I suggest that clients throw themselves an *"I'm Worthless Party"* after they've worked hard to achieve their "$0" net worth. (Just don't put the party on a credit card that you can't pay off next month!)

Ignore the urge to put your head in the sand thinking you have no power over the situation. *You are not alone and there's no reason to be embarrassed.* To prove it you can take a look at our government. Their high federal deficit sets a dangerous precedent not only for our culture but also the world's economy. No matter how big your debt problem, it looks relatively small in this light!

Simply make up your mind now to reverse the situation and be proud that you're taking the right steps. The obvious way to improve your net worth is to decrease your spending and/or increase your income and investments. Begin by taking a serious look at your spending habits and make sure that you are doing everything you can to achieve, first a zero, and eventually a positive, net worth. Getting yourself back to financial stability may feel like a long and lonely road, but with the help of a financial planner you at least don't have to feel like you're going it alone.

The Millionaire Next Door by Thomas Stanley outlines some benchmark figures for what your net worth should be at any given time, age or stage in life. Your net worth represents your financial security and ultimately, financial independence. So of course, the closer you are to retirement, the higher your net worth should be. A successful financial plan achieves one's maximum net worth, works under all circumstances, and maximizes the enjoyment of your wealth. It will also be important to insure yourself against unforeseen tragedies and to consider whether you want to leave an inheritance to your family or your favorite charity, leaving behind a legacy that lives on after you.

In summary, the most critical starting point to a financial plan is evaluating your net worth. Then, on a periodic basis, you can compare the results in order to establish trends and measure improvement. A convenient time to do this is once a year when you're doing your taxes. This way all the paperwork is readily available and you're focused on your annual earnings and expenditures. Keep all the financial records together from each year's tax forms and net worth calculations for easy reference.

Your Budget

After calculating your net worth, you'll want to look at your monthly budget and define exactly where your money is being spent. The categories of the monthly budget should also include any deductions from your paycheck like state and federal income taxes, Social Security and employee benefits. Once you have your take home pay you should deduct all of the fixed expenses and the estimated variable expenses.

Are you unable to account for where a large portion of your money goes? This is the case for many people. To overcome it, try a few or all of the following tips.

- Carry a pocket calendar with you for three months and record every cent that you spend, no matter if it's for a candy bar or cup of coffee, or the mortgage and car payment. Then tally it up and categorize it at the end of each month (some software programs, like *Quicken*, make this very easy) in order to see exactly where your paychecks are going.

- Vow to go back to the days of *cash only* transactions. For everything other than your large monthly payments (and even those if you want to get really serious), stop using your debit and credit cards or writing checks for day-to-day expenditures like groceries, drugstore items, clothing, etc. It feels much different when you have to shell out $50 cash for a purchase than handing over a piece of plastic.

- Treat your savings account or investment amount as a bill that you pay out every month like any other. Experience has shown that if you don't get in the habit of saving money on a regular basis, either through a payroll deduction or an automatic withdrawal from you checking account, the money you intended to go toward savings or investments is mysteriously spent elsewhere.

How quickly you can move toward financial security depends on how motivated you are to saving money. It's not easy for Americans to live on less than their income considering our credit-loving culture. However, if you start early enough, saving 15 percent of your gross income will typically be enough to keep you safe from financial worries later on. If you are getting a later start, then you may need to be living on 75-80 percent of your income and saving 20-25 percent!

Saving or investing this amount means you are able to live on 85 percent of your income. As elementary as this may sound, the significance is critical. In later years, this savings could accumulate to a substantial sum if invested properly. Also, it will teach you how to live below your means—a financial goal that seemingly every expert agrees upon, but few Americans live by.

3

The Pyramid

If you took a jigsaw puzzle and dumped all the pieces on the table, it is initially a daunting task to begin to put the puzzle together. Take a puzzle piece out of the pile at random, and it's hard to know where that piece fits into the big picture. It is much easier to put the puzzle together if you have a picture of what the scene will look like once completed. So, you look at the picture on the box to give you a guide to what the puzzle looks like when completed. I designed the pyramid as a method of seeing how a properly designed financial plan looks when it is put together correctly.

The pyramid is a method of explaining the financial planning concept by categorizing your financial plan into stages. Of course, individual goals, habits, accomplishments, etc. are all unique, but most people share the same fundamental life stages. As a method of simply and efficiently organizing your financial life, the pyramid represents the key to financial independence, and demonstrates the basic goal of increasing your assets and reducing your debt in order to have enough money invested to retire comfortably. Individuals may place more or less importance on one section of the pyramid than another, which is perfectly acceptable.

Without a doubt, organizing your finances in order to build a solid base is the first step. If you do this, you may be subjecting your financial situation to undue risk, which will cause problems later on. On the other hand, it's also important not to place too much emphasis on only one stage, neglecting the overall balance. This could be a sign of being overly conservative. As an example, not taking advantage of higher potential returns in equity (stock) investments may mean losing your purchasing power in the long run, because the dollars may be worth less due to the effects of taxes and inflation.

It is very important to try and accomplish a lifelong financial balance. You certainly don't want to get to the age of 65 with a huge amount of money saved up, only to be in poor health and not be able to enjoy it, especially if that means you scrimped and saved your whole life and worked so hard that you didn't enjoy yourself along the way. By the same token, you don't want to be nearing retirement and realize you haven't saved enough and now must take a substantial drop in your standard of living or go back to work to simply survive. The ideal situation would be to retire at the same or a greater standard of living than that you were accustomed to in your working years, but not feel at any time that you have greatly sacrificed.

A fundamental of short and long-term financial success is living on less that your income. If you can get used to living on 80-90 percent of your income, this allows you to commit 10-20 percent of your income to your net worth. Initially, this may mean aggressively paying of loans, but over time, the majority of this extra income should be saved. If you are living paycheck to paycheck, is there a way you can decrease your expenses, and/or increase your income so that you can start building some surplus funds into your monthly budget?

As you can see by the diagram, there are four main stages to the financial planning pyramid: *The Security and Confidence Stage, The Capital Accumulation Stage,* and *The Tax-Advantaged Stage and the Speculation Stage.*

PYRAMID OF FINANCIAL NEEDS

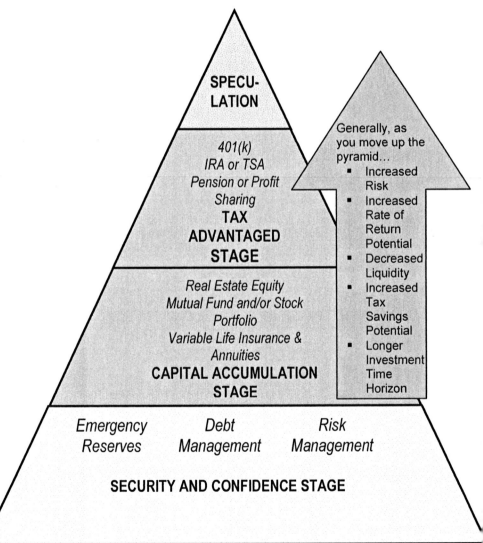

The ideal investment is completely liquid, has lots of tax advantages and a great rate of return and low risk. If you find an advisor or salesman claiming to have such an investment, you would be wise avoid them as they are dangerous. This ideal investment does not exist. Let's use an analogy of spinning plates. If you have ever been to a circus or seen a juggler, you may have seen a performer attempt to spin a lot of plates on long sticks....all at the same time. The objective is to take limited energy, and allocate it in such a manner as to keep all the plates spinning. It doesn't do any good to devote a lot of time to one spinning plate while the others are slowing down, wobbling and falling down. The goal is to keep all the plates spinning!

Your financial plan is on somewhat the same level, with each financial decision representing a different plate. First of all, you need to find out which plates you want to start spinning and then direct your dollars to keep them going. You could have several debt reduction plates, some risk management (insurance) plates, retirement and/or college education plates, and so on. Each individual situation is going to be different. Again, there are limited resources that need to be allocated in such a way as to accomplish all of your goals. This is where the advice of a professional and experienced financial advisor can be very valuable.

The key financial variables in the pyramid are risk, liquidity, rate of return and tax advantages. The money in your emergency reserves and at the *Security and Confidence Stage* should be very liquid or accessible. Generally, as you move to higher stages in the pyramid, the less liquid your funds become.

Risk and rate of return tend to go hand in hand. The higher the amount of risk you take, the higher the rate of return should be......given time. In the pyramid, typically lower risk with lower rates of return should be at the base of your planning and the risk and rate of return increase as you move up the pyramid. Historically, stock market and investing returns become more predictable the longer the time frame that is considered. Keep it mind, however, that past performance is not indicative of future results.

From a tax standpoint, there are typically not too many tax advantages at the lower level. If you have money in a savings account, that money is generating ordinary income on which you are paying tax, so there are no tax advantages there. On the other hand, when you put money into a qualified retirement plan, the contribution is on a before tax basis, delaying and deferring the tax to a later date. Under most circumstances, however, you cannot touch the money in your qualified plan until age 59½ without paying a 10 percent early withdrawal penalty, plus the income taxes due on that amount. The rule of thumb on tax savings is similar to risk and rate of return. As you move up the pyramid, you'll have greater tax advantages on your investments.

A Discussion of Risk

There is no such thing as a risk-free investment, even a savings account is not risk free. Let me explain. Risk is commonly discussed in terms of loss of principal. Most recently, during the recent bear market (a period of downturn in the stock market), many investors lost some of the value of their investment if they owned stocks and/or stock mutual funds. There are other forms of risk besides market risk.

Purchasing Power Risk: Another term for this is inflation. If the cost for products and services rises faster than the interest rate being credited on your savings and checking accounts, then you are exposed to purchasing power risk. While you don't lose any principal, you are still losing ground relative to inflation. This is a particular problem currently for retirees who have traditionally held CDs and lived off the interest each year.

Interest Rate Risk: Bonds and Fixed Income securities are subject to this risk. Your principal value can decline if interest rates climb quickly. The severity of the loss is often magnified by the duration and/or maturity of the bonds and the credit quality. At this time, when interest rates are near forty-year lows, many people who own fixed income securities are unknowingly subjecting their investments to interest rate risk.

Business Risk: This is the risk of losing money due to circumstances out of your control. A business could go bankrupt, and your investment becomes worthless.

Liquidity Risk: This is the risk associated with being invested in real estate, limited partnerships, businesses and other investments where there is sometimes no immediate market for your value. This is problematic if you have a need for cash and you cannot sell or liquidate your shares. You would invest in something like this only if you had sufficient assets available besides this investment.

Regulatory Risk: Investors run the risk that government policy decisions or influences of society as a whole could endanger an investment's value. Environmental and tax legislation can have a dramatic impact on certain investment values, up or down. It is important to note this risk when investing.

Currency Risk: An investment in international securities can be affected by foreign exchange rate changes, political and economic instability, as well as differences in accounting standards.

Diversity Risk: This will be discussed at length later in the book, but allow me to overstate the obvious......DIVERSIFY!

In summary, a properly structured financial plan will balance all of these variables so that you are diversified by asset class, risk levels, tax treatment, and time horizon.

4

The Security and Confidence Stage

This stage is divided into three main sections with an emphasis on building up emergency reserves, making sure debt is under control and taking care of risk management (insurance) needs. Each of these factors is equally important. Most people agree on the need to have money accessible for emergencies, to pay their debts, especially on high interest credit cards, and to be adequately insured. The trick to the individual financial plan is to figure out the appropriate level for each of these.

Does your financial agenda resemble that of Will Rogers as he said:

"I'm not so much concerned about the rate of return on my money, just the return of it."

1. Emergency Reserves:

The one constant in life is that there will always be surprises. The purpose of an emergency reserve fund is just what it sounds like—money that is very accessible when you really need it. The main characteristic of an investment in this category would be the money that is liquid, yet safely invested so the principal remains intact. The most common mistake people make here is not having adequate reserves or taking undue risk with these funds. This money needs to remain liquid in case of unexpected expenses, like the car expenses, home repairs, job loss or medical emergencies, etc. For most people, peace of mind is the main benefit of having an adequate emergency reserve fund. When you are financially prepared for these surprises, they become less stressful and are therefore easier to deal with emotionally. Furthermore, when there is a source of funds for these types of emergencies you do not have to rely on credit cards, or personal unsecured high interest loans.

As a general rule of thumb, your emergency reserve account would be able to cover approximately three months of bills. So, if your monthly expenses are averaging $3,000, then your emergency reserve fund should be $9,000. Of course, this is a rough guide and you may want to consider having a higher emergency reserve if you anticipate a big purchase, such as a car or home. Ideally, you do not want to deplete your emergency reserve completely in order to purchase such items.

It may also be important to consider an *emotional rule of thumb*—at what point would a drop in your emergency reserves make you feel nervous? Or, said another way, what is the minimum level of cash that you need to have? This amount differs for everyone and should take into consideration the stability of your job, your equity in a home, how large and/or liquid your other investments are, and any large bills or purchases you may be planning. If a large purchase or unexpected expenses do drain your reserves, then the emphasis of your financial plan should be to replenish those funds at a higher priority than your other investments.

The typical investments that can be used to hold your emergency reserves would include bank investments, money market funds, and/or insurance cash values. The common theme among these investments is their liquidity and the safety of the principal. If you use a bank for your emergency reserves, typically these funds are in savings accounts and interest-bearing checking accounts, as well as money market funds.

For safety of principal and liquidity, savings accounts are the most common option, but not necessarily the best. Such accounts are insured so there is no market risk, but lots of purchasing poser risk. But, this also means there is typically a lower yield than other investments.

Another option is a CD (certificate of deposit), with a relatively short maturity. The disadvantage to a CD is that the money is tied up for a certain length of time and removing the funds sooner will result in an interest rate penalty. To avoid this problem, it can make sense to stagger your CD maturities so that you always have some that come due every six months or so. Therefore, you can access it if you need to or reinvest if you don't.

A money market mutual fund is often the best choice as an emergency reserve possibility. Many people incorrectly associate the term mutual fund with high risk. However, a mutual fund only has as much risk as the underlying investments it owns. A money market mutual fund pools investors' dollars in the typical mutual fund style, and purchases jumbo CDs through banks, Treasury securities (T bills), as well as commercial paper. Most money market funds have a check writing privilege, which allows you to write checks against your account, subject to minimums of usually $250 or $500. The rate of return earned on these funds will fluctuate based on the short-term money market, but is typically competitive with the interest rate at the time. Investments in a money market fund are neither insured nor guaranteed by the FDIC, or any government agency. Although the fund seeks to preserve the value of your investment at $1.00 per share, it is possible to lose money by investing in the fund.

Life insurance cash values on permanent policies (i.e. whole life, adjustable life, universal life) can also be important sources of emergency reserve funds. These funds are typically earning a competitive fixed rate of return and they are accessible. It is usually possible to take out a loan or borrow against your cash value, using it as collateral; or sometimes you can take an outright withdrawal of this money. Remember, though, that any loans or withdrawals taken will reduce both your policy cash value and death benefit.

A home equity line of credit is another option. If you have equity in your house, and if interest rates are low and these loans are tax deductible, this option should not be discounted. In fact, in periods of time when there is a low interest rate environment, maintaining an open line of credit against your house equity is my favorite form of a source of emergency reserve cash. It could also be used to pay down a high interest credit card or for a major purchase, like a car. The drawback is that it needs to be paid off when you sell your house, which of course would result in less proceeds at closing.

2. Debt Management

If you are in the fortunate situation of having no debts, congratulations! If you come from the school of thought that you don't ever want to owe anything to anybody, debt management is not an issue. However, in today's society this ideology is very uncommon and many people could use some strategies on effectively managing their debt.

Financially, it would make sense to rank all of your debts from highest to lowest interest, paying attention to the after-tax cost of borrowing. Since consumer debt is not tax deductible, those rates are taken at face value. However, a mortgage or home equity loan is deductible, so the real rate of return is the after-tax cost.

To give another general rule of thumb, credit cards and consumer debt would be the first to pay off, if they have the highest interest rates. Then you would want to work away at the furniture loan, the used car loan, the new car loan, student loans, and finally, the home mortgage. Nowadays there are many credit cards that offer very low interest rates on balance transfers, which can be a temporary solution. But beware that the rate after the introductory period is not actually higher than your current card.

It is also important to look at debt management from a cash flow standpoint as well as an emotional standpoint. With this in mind, it can make sense to pay off a lower interest loan if it will improve your cash flow dramatically, or emotionally it is important for you to get it paid off for some other reason. Many people find a sense of satisfaction in paying debts off completely. Once one debt is paid off, take the extra cash and immediately begin paying off another loan more aggressively, so that cash does not get absorbed into the budget.

Check your credit report. It's a good idea to review your credit report every year. The financial information included in this report will have a bearing on whether you can obtain a loan, auto or home insurance, rent an apartment, or even apply for a job. Contact the credit bureaus and correct any errors you find. I would suggest starting at www.experian.com.

3. Risk Management

Protecting yourself against unforeseen catastrophic losses is the third critical area of the base of the pyramid and the Security and Confidence Stage. In fact, think of this as a three-legged stool. Kick one leg out and the stool will not stand. The financial pyramid is just like that.

Important insurance coverage can include health and major medical, auto, disability, long-term care and homeowners or renters. In many cases, life and/or disability insurance are overlooked. However, these can be very important depending on your personal situation.

The reason for placing risk management at this point is obvious. You need to protect yourself from losses that would create such a hole that you may otherwise never dig yourself out. Then, once you are on your way to financial independence, insurance plays an equally important role in protecting your assets.

While you don't want to have any gaps in your insurance protection, you certainly don't want to overlap or duplicate coverage. The ideal financial plan will have you paying reasonable premium levels while providing maximum protection. Remember, the major role of insurance is to protect against catastrophic losses. A common mistake is trying to insure too many contingencies or not using deductibles to your advantage.

You will want to ask yourself a couple of questions before purchasing insurance:

- *Is the premium for this coverage going to dramatically affect my lifestyle?*
- *If I do not buy this coverage and suffer the losses that would have been covered, would I be in grave financial trouble?*

If the answer to the first question is *no* and to the second *yes*, then the insurance in question is right for you. If not, reconsider the structure and price of the insurance. Consult an experienced financial professional to help you determine the appropriate levels of coverage and how to structure your insurance within the context of a comprehensive financial plan.   .

When it comes to life insurance it is easy to become confused. Some complicated terminology like *term life, whole life, universal life, variable whole life,* etc. may put you off, but by understanding just a few terms and some of the benefits and disadvantages, you will be much more prepared to evaluate the coverage that is best for you. If structured correctly, life insurance can be one of the most versatile and powerful financial tools available.

- *Term life:* While the premiums are low for the young, the price increases dramatically as you get older. Although young couples with children may find term life insurance to be the only affordable option, it is important to remember that this option brings *no investment benefits.* To optimize value on the policy a *guaranteed renewal clause* allows for renewal to the policy without a medical requalification. Another value-adding option is a clause, which allows a conversion from a renewable term policy to a permanent policy without proof of insurability.
- *Whole life:* The most appealing feature of whole life insurance is its unchanging premium and guaranteed long-term coverage. Also, it builds up a tax-deferred "cash value." The cash value is what the insurer will return on cancellation of the policy. But, whole life costs more than term life initially. Some critics believe whole life's cash value grows too slowly and as an investment option the buyer is better off buying term insurance and investing the difference in the stock market. The policies' rates of returns today are much more

competitive than in the past, and this can be a very viable policy for a portion of your financial plan.

- *Adjustable/universal life*: The main feature of this policy is the flexibility in initial design and the ability to change as your needs change. If money gets tight, with this type of policy it's possible to lower the annual premium. You can also increase or decrease the death benefit as your needs change. Typically, increases in death benefit require additional proof of insurability.

- *Variable Life*: The cash values are invested into investment sub-accounts with your choice of the allocation to stocks, bonds and/or money markets. The policy's cash value and death benefit can increase if the investments do well. But, the opposite could also occur. Look ahead to the next chapter for a more advanced discussion of this type of policy.

Disability insurance is one of the most important and overlooked types of insurance coverage. The odds of a long-term disability (lasting 90 days or longer) are six to seven times greater than a death during working years. While many employers provide group disability insurance, the benefits are generally 60 percent of one's income and taxable. The net effect is that only 40-45 percent of your income is protected.

Remember, you get what you pay for. Searching the internet for the cheapest insurance policy often results in coverage that will not protect you and your family adequately. A competent insurance agent or financial planner can provide a valuable service and should be used. They can be the best resource in helping you to select adequate coverage at appropriate prices and at claim time they can help you decipher the paperwork. Choosing someone you trust, especially someone who comes recommended from a reliable source, will prove invaluable. Also, there may be some other aspects of your overall financial plan, which if reworked, can help you to maximize your insurance protection, while building wealth for the future using better strategies than you were aware of.

As your assets grow, it is wise to expand your umbrella liability insurance coverage. The limits built into most homeowners and auto policies are minimal. This coverage actually protects your assets in the event you or a family member cause harm due to your negligence. In addition, be sure to ask your agent for excess umbrella liability coverage for uninsured/underinsured motorists. This coverage protects you and your family for negligent acts caused by others.

In many cases, insurance is thought of as a "necessary evil." You have to have it but it only benefits you if you have a claim. I look at the insurance coverage I own as a valuable part of an overall comprehensive financial plan. The peace of mind I have by knowing my family and I are covered is worth a lot. In addition, I can be more aggressive with my other savings and investments, because I know that my risk management needs are taken care of.

Looking back to the middle ages, we get a glimpse of the importance of insurance. People of wealth built fabulous castles and filled them with treasures. They always devoted significant resources to protecting those assets in the form of an army, a moat, etc. In a sense, that was an early form of an insurance policy. So, as you continue to build your net worth, you should review and update your insurance to be sure you are maximizing your coverage and protecting you and your family and your wealth.

5

The Capital Accumulation Stage

This stage represents a large amount of assets that you will build up over your lifetime. The assets that tend to comprise this stage are quite varied. Some of the investments include individual stocks and bonds, mutual funds, variable life insurance cash values, and equity in real estate or in a business. Aside from the equity that you build into your retirement plan, the majority of your financial independence will come from these investments. While these assets can also serve as emergency reserves, the investment horizon is usually five years or longer.

Keep in mind that all investments have risk. However, there are varying degrees and types of risk. The risk most often associated with an investment involves a fluctuating principal or a sudden depreciation in the stock market, as in October 1987, or the bear market of 2000-2002. A corporate bond or government security holds the risk of loss of principal due to an increase in interest rates. Even a safe investment in a money market fund has purchasing power risk, because after taxes and inflation are figured in, your dollars could be worth less than when you originally invested. A summary of the types of risk is found towards the end of Chapter Three.

Saving money is one of the most important criteria in assuring financial success. Get in the habit now of saving between 10-20 percent of your gross income. By living below your total income, even to this small degree, not only will your money be worth more in the long run by wisely investing it, you will also cultivate a responsible attitude toward your money. Keeping up with the Jones has become a national epidemic. But the real truth is the millionaires next door don't concern themselves with flaunting their wealth, which explains why they are wealthy.

Variable life policies are becoming increasingly popular. Because of their unique investment opportunities, their tax deferral potential and their excellent rates of return potential, this new type of insurance policy should be examined by anyone who is investing money at the *Capital Accumulation Stage*. Such policies allow an individual to purchase a single financial instrument providing for both life insurance and long-term accumulation goals. They often serve as a form of "forced investment" for those who find it difficult to put funds aside on a regular basis, but who routinely pay their bills. Obviously, your level of insurance needs and wants has a large bearing on how the policy is structured and it's important to carefully structure loans and withdrawals to avoid negative income tax results.

For many Americans, one of the most substantial forms of saving is simply making a monthly payment on your home. Generally speaking, real estate has long been a favorite investment tool for its tax benefits and as a buffer against inflation. Although there can be significant investment benefits in the long term, buying real estate is not without its risks. Deflation may decrease property values or suspected long-term growth in a given area may not occur. Changes in tax law may reduce or eliminate anticipated tax benefits. Also, real estate is not liquid, so the necessity of a quick sale may require a substantial reduction in price.

The term "stock" or "share" both refer to a partial ownership interest in a corporation, or equity. As a stockholder you'll be able to vote for the company's Board of Directors, and receive information on the firm's activities and business results. You may share in "dividends" or current profits.

Investors typically buy and hold stock for its long-term growth potential. Stocks with a history of regular dividends are often held for both income and growth. As the long-term growth of a company cannot be predicted, the short-term market value of the company's stock will fluctuate up and down. If your financial need or your fear causes you to sell when the market is "down" (also called a "bear market"), a capital loss can result. If the market is "up" (also called a "bull market"), the investor can realize a capital gain when selling.

While stocks represent ownership in a business, bonds are debt issued by institutions such as the federal government, corporations, and state and local governments. At the bonds' "maturity," the principal amount will be returned. In the meantime, bond holders receive interest. When first issued, a bond will have a specified interest rate, or "yield." If a bond is traded on a public exchange, the market price will fluctuate, generally with changes in interest rates.

Using a mutual fund is an excellent way to lower your risk, because you are diversifying through a number of stocks. A properly designed mutual fund portfolio is generally the most appropriate method of accumulating wealth at this point in the financial pyramid. Some funds have high "market risk," meaning they can fluctuate quite dramatically. Past experience shows that funds that have the most risk have upside and downside potential that needs to be carefully considered. Funds with low market risk often have "inflation risk." These funds usually produce lower returns which may not keep up with inflation.

If your investment horizon is relatively short (up to five years), then a more conservatively balanced fund, equity income fund, or even a medium-term corporate bond or government securities fund, will likely be the most appropriate. When your investment horizon is longer, growth-oriented stock funds are generally going to be the best choice. Again, each circumstance is different and the advice of a competent professional will be valuable. Most firms have a short investment attitude questionnaire which you can answer to help you determine the appropriate asset allocation strategy that meets your needs.

Diversify! Diversify! Diversify! Nothing else will be as crucial to your portfolio as diversifying and having a long-term vision. It's important to diversity not only by asset class but also by tax treatment and time horizon. We all know the proverb "Don't put all your eggs in one basket." Well, take it to the extreme—don't put all the baskets on the same truck and don't drive all the trucks down the same road! It's not necessary to look too far back to recall the faddish investing in technology and start-up companies of the late 1990s. Too many investors lost too much when the overvalued stocks plunged and those eager investors expecting big returns were left with substantial losses.

Sometimes misunderstood, the main goal of diversification is not to maximize your return, but to minimize your risk and lower your volatility. The basic premise is that there is as much risk in being out of the market when it goes up as being in the market when it goes down, especially for your long-term money. As an example, take the period between 1926 and 1995, a period of 840 months; if you were out of the market during the 30 top performing months—about 3.6 percent of the time—you would have ended up with a return similar to Treasury Bills! While diversification does not guarantee against loss, it is a method used to manage risk.

Some additional strategies to employ when investing include dollar cost averaging and portfolio rebalancing. Dollar cost averaging is the process of investing a fixed amount of money each month (or quarter, or year) without worrying about whether the market is up or down. When it is down, you will buy more shares, bringing your average share price down. Over time, besides the element of forced savings, you will hopefully see returns that you are happy with. Dollar cost averaging does not assure a profit, nor does it protect against loss in declining markets. This investment strategy requires regular investments regardless of the fluctuating price of the investment. You should consider your financial ability to continue investing through periods of low price levels.

When there is a large amount of money to invest, coming up with an investment policy and adhering to it is a must. Once an overall asset allocation mix is chosen based on your goals and objectives, stick to it and change only if there are significant changes in the economy, the portfolio, and/or your goals and objectives. Then, on a regular basis, either quarterly, semiannually, or annually, rebalance the portfolio back to the asset allocation you had started with. With this strategy, your investment mix does not get skewed towards more or less risk and volatility. Many current portfolio managers have the capability of providing this rebalancing process on an automatic basis.

A well-balanced portfolio is properly diversified by the following asset decisions:

-Stocks versus bonds
-US (domestic) investment versus International securities
-Large Cap versus small cap stocks
-Growth versus value stocks (keep this in balance!)

There are many good resources to turn to that will help you take this process much further than the scope of this book. Some of those are found in Chapter Eight. I think some of the best information can come from a competent and qualified financial advisor who will listen to you and develop a plan that meets your needs.

In general, a higher investment risk is best for those who:

- can accept short-term losses;
- believe gains will offset losses over the long run;
- will not leave the investment if one or two bad years occur;
- have a long "investment time horizon."

The best way to learn sound market advice is to listen to the experts. The following quotes from mutual fund leaders all stress the futility of market timing:

Peter Lynch: *"My single-most important piece of investment advice is to ignore the short-term fluctuations of the market. From one year to the next, the stock market is a coin flip. It can go up or down. The real money in stocks is made in the third, fourth and fifth year of your investments, because you are participating in a company's earnings which grow over time."*

Warren Buffet: *"I do not have, never have had, and never will have an opinion where the stock market will be a year from now."*

Sir John Templeton: *"Ignore fluctuations. Do not try to outguess the stock market. Buy a quality portfolio and invest for the long term."*

So, to drive it home, *invest for the long term and be patient!*

6

The Tax-Advantaged Stage

The main thrust of this stage is to try to significantly delay, reduce and/or minimize the impact of taxes on your financial picture. Why? To accumulate and create the highest net worth you possibly can. One method of delaying the tax involves investing dollars into qualified retirement plans. This means that the dollars are made on a before tax (qualified) basis. Again, the taxes are not eliminated, they are just deferred until the funds are withdrawn. These plans include individual retirement accounts (IRAs), simplified employee pensions (SEPs), tax-sheltered annuities (TSAs), pension and profit sharing plans, 401k plans, etc.

The main advantage behind these plans is that the government has given you a significant motivation to save money because your taxable income is reduced dollar for dollar by the contribution, which will then save you anywhere from 10-35 percent of the deposit in taxes. In other words your adjusted gross income is less, which means your taxable income is reduced. While these accounts are good places to defer and delay the tax liability during your working years, they present some problems at retirement because of the tax due then. And, transferring qualified assets to heirs can present some tax nightmares if not handled carefully.

The general principal here is to save money into these plans when you are in a higher tax bracket, and withdraw the funds at retirement when you are in a lower tax bracket. I do see some problems, though. In some cases, when a person is early in their career, and the income and tax bracket is low, it doesn't make any sense to put a lot of money into an IRA or 401k. Why defer money when you are in the lowest tax bracket you will ever be in? Instead, you may want to contribute to the 401k just up to where the employer matches those funds, but then again, only if you plan to be at that job for a few years to become vested (the employer's matching funds are yours if you are vested when you leave), and have taken care of the Security and Confidence Stage of your financial plan.

The reason the *Tax-Advantaged Stage* belongs above the *Capital Accumulation* and *Security & Confidence Stages* of the pyramid is because the money deposited into these plans is normally not available until you reach the age of 59 ½. There are methods of getting your money out early, by borrowing the funds, or if disabled, or have a hardship situation, but for the most part money flowing into these plans should be regarded as retirement money that cannot be touched until then.

Calculating Your Tax Bracket

Just for you, I have taken the 10,000 page tax code and narrowed it down to two pages (see pages 57 and 58). Wouldn't that be nice if preparing our taxes was that easy! This is, of course, a basic guide only, just for education purposes, and doesn't factor in some of the specifics such as child care, student loan interest deductions, moving expenses, etc. But, surprisingly, this is fairly accurate in estimating the federal tax liability.

I encourage working with your accountant, running one of the tax software packages, or simply using this guide any time you have a major change in your life that will affect your taxes. Family changes such as a birth, death, or a marriage all affect the tax that you owe. Financial changes such as a new job, a raise, going back to school, buying or moving to a new house will also impact your tax liability, and a new calculation should be made. Compare your calculation to the amount you are having withheld from your paycheck, and if you are withholding too much, change this with your employer by filling out a new W-4 form.

This is especially useful for a student graduating in May or June and starting employment mid-year. If you don't work with your employer on the correct tax withholding, they will take out an amount that would correspond to you working for the whole year. Generally, there are many expenses and having a higher tax home pay would most likely be more beneficial than getting a tax refund the following spring.

There are some important basic points to understand about taxes. First, getting a large refund isn't really all that smart. It means that you just gave the government an interest free loan for the year. If you are a terrible saver and use this as a forced savings plan, I'm guessing it still backfires on you because you know the lump sum tax refund is coming and you have plans for spending that amount too! In any event, I suggest that you estimate your tax liability in advance and try to end up about even. That avoids any underwitholding penalties, and also any unexpected tax liability due that you may not be prepared for.

The second point is that it is always in your best interest to make more money! I've heard people say: "I just got a raise (or a bonus, or whatever) and it jumped me into the next tax bracket, so I'm going to take home less!" That's not how it works. The tax system is a progressive tax and the more income you make, the more you take home. It's just that each additional dollar is taxed at a higher percentage, but the first dollars are taxed the same. Repeated, moving into a higher tax bracket affects the last of your dollars you earn, but the first dollars are still taxed at the same rate.

As an example, let's look at the Basic Federal Tax Estimator on the next page. Plug in your income (wages, interest income, etc) and subtract contributions to pretax accounts to get your adjusted gross income. From that, you subtract your personal exemptions and either the standard deduction or your itemized deductions, whichever is higher. Then, look up your tax bracket on the chart. The tax bracket is the tax on each additional dollar you earn, or the tax that is saved by virtue of reducing your taxable income by a dollar.

Suppose you are single and your taxable income happens to be exactly $68,600. Your best friend's taxable income comes in at $68,801, or $1 more. Bummer for them, right? Yes and no. Their tax liability is only 28 cents more than yours, because each new dollar is taxed at the 28 percent rate. They still have a take home pay of 72 cents more than you, so while at a higher tax bracket, their take home pay is more. The total tax is calculated as follows:

First $7,000 of taxable income: $700 ($7,000 x .1)
Next $21,400 of taxable income $3,210 ($21,400 x .15)
Next $40,399 of taxable income $10,100 ($40,399 x .25)
Total Tax: $14,100

Your friend's tax bill would be calculated the same as yours with another 28 of tax liability on the $1 above $68,800 at the 28 percent tax bracket. Work through your own situation a few times and this should be easier to understand.

Basic Federal Tax Estimator

(This is a guide only. This does not factor in child care, student loan interest deductions, medical expenses, moving, etc.)

Gross Income: *Wages, Interest income, etc.*

Minus: **Adjustments:** *IRA, 401(k), TSA,* —
etc.   -

Equals: **Adjusted Gross Income (AGI)**   =
                                                              ___

Minus:

     Personal Exemptions ($3,050 x # in household)   -
     (Phased out as income exceeds certain limits)

And the higher of: ___

     Standard Deduction (Single - $4,750; Married -   -
     $9,500)

                                                             ___

Or

     Itemized Deductions

         • State Income Tax

- Home Mortgage Interest and Property Tax

- Charitable Contributions

Equals: **Taxable Income**   =

                                                              ___

Federal Income Tax Due: (See Tax Table Below)

2003 Individual Income Tax Rates

Single				Married Filing Jointly			
$	- to	7,000	10.00%	$	- to	14,000	10.00%
7,001	to	28,400	15.00%	14,001	to	56,800	15.00%
28,401	to	68,800	25.00%	56,801	to	114,650	25.00%
68,801	to	143,500	28.00%	114,651	to	174,700	28.00%
143,501	to	311,950	33.00%	174,701	to	311,950	33.00%
311,951	-		35.00%	311,951	-		35.00%

There are substantial tax benefits with a variety of non-qualified investments also. The term non-qualified means that there is no immediate tax deduction when contributing to these accounts, but the tax benefits can be more beneficial over your lifetime. The following assets are generally part of the capital accumulation stage, but I'll provide the discussion of the tax reduction strategy of each technique in this chapter.

Stocks: As stocks appreciate in value (for this discussion, we'll assume they appreciate!) there is no tax due on the appreciation until the stock is sold. Along the way, if any dividends are paid, the tax rate is less (15 percent for the highest tax bracket) than the ordinary income tax rate. In addition, when the stock is sold, if held for over a year, the gain is taxed at the lower 15 percent capital gain rate. So, there is a benefit of tax deferral during the holding period and tax minimizing due to the gain being treated as a capital gain.

Roth IRAs: Assuming you have all of your Security and Confidence Stage issues taken care of, and your income is such that you can use Roth IRAs, I would recommend it. You do not get a current tax deduction, but under current law, all the growth (again...assuming it grows!) is tax deferred. Then, when you take the money out of the Roth IRA at retirement, you receive it tax free. Would you rather pay tax on the seeds going into the ground, or the end of the year harvest? Growth in a Roth IRA may not be withdrawn until the later of reaching age 59½ or maintaining your Roth IRA for a period of five years. Withdrawals prior to this are subject to a 10 percent early withdrawal penalty.

Real Estate: Real estate can be an excellent method of building wealth. Getting away from rent and into your first home is one obvious way. Another is leveraging the equity you have in your existing real estate into additional property. The growth is tax deferred and there are some favorable strategies available upon the sale and/or disposition. As for financing your house, contrary to popular belief, it can make sense to put little money down and stretch the mortgage out (and the tax deduction) in favor of freeing up cash flow for other goals and objectives. For a comprehensive discussion of this topic, I'd encourage you to pick up Doug Andrew's book, *Missed Fortune*.

Life Insurance: The benefits of a life insurance policy are much like those of the Roth IRA, with some additional features. As an accumulation tool, there is a cost for the insurance, so this is appropriate for someone who is younger and in good health and has a longer investment time horizon. The cash values grow tax deferred and can be accessed tax free, if structured properly. It is generally best to avoid having the policy become a Modified Endowment Policy (MEC) and working with a very knowledgeable insurance or financial professional is a must.

Having a permanent life insurance policy can help you maximize your overall net worth in some other ways, too. You reduce your need for term insurance, which frees up cash. In fact, the most beneficial time to have a permanent life insurance policy in place is at retirement because of all of the advantages it provides. Briefly, you can be more aggressive in using and enjoying your other assets because the life insurance essentially provides a "permission slip" to do so. Work with your financial advisor to coordinate this with your overall financial plan.

State Sponsored 529 College Plans: There are a number of methods of putting investments in your children or grandchildren's name. If the funds are ultimately to help them with their future college education expenses, a 529 plan is the answer. Some states allow a state tax deduction on the contributions and all of the plans grow tax deferred. If the funds are withdrawn for tuition, room and board and "qualifying" education needs, the funds can be withdrawn tax free also. These funds can even be transferred between family members. For a lengthier discussion, as well as a link to your state sponsored plan, go to www.savingforcollege.com. However, make sure that your own financial security is assured and your financial pyramid is sound before aggressively putting money into your children's accounts.

Annuities: An annuity is marketed by an insurance company as their answer to other investments. There are numerous benefits of non-qualified annuities as another financial instrument. Namely, they grow tax deferred, you can switch between the separate accounts in a variable annuity without tax implications, and there are some death benefit guarantees to protect the value for your heirs. Withdrawals from annuities prior to age 59½ are subject to a 10 percent early withdrawal penalty, as well as potential deferred sales charges.

What Do You Do At Retirement?

Estimating your retirement needs is an important factor to consider at this stage of the pyramid. A financial planning rule of thumb is to figure on needing 70 percent to 80 percent of your pre-retirement income, although more and more people are enjoying a retirement lifestyle that is close to their working years. This figure should be based on the income you plan to be earning at retirement, not that which you're making today. To estimate this, look at your current expenses and subtract the expenses and savings that will not be needed at retirement, and add in extra expenses (travel, medical, etc.) that may be needed then. Consider the following:

- Will you still be paying a mortgage?
- Do you anticipate hefty medical expenses for yourself or spouse?

- Do you wish to travel extensively?
- Will your day-to-day living expenses be similar, or less, than what they are now?

If your budget allows, and you have your Security and Confidence Stage taken care of, then take full advantage of any 401 (k) or similar plans your employer offers, at least up until the amount that the employer matches. This type of retirement investment defers tax payment on the contributed earnings until the money is withdrawn, usually at retirement. If your employer matches any of your contribution, this is an added tax benefit.

If you are self-employed, then consider a Simplified Employee Pension (SEP) or SIMPLE retirement plan, which also allows you to take advantage of the pre-tax growth that has been described in this chapter. Deciding on the correct retirement plan will be something that a competent financial advisor can help you with.

7

The Speculation Stage

The speculation stage involves risking money that you can afford to lose. Some people are never comfortable with this and thus should not consider it. These people should simply build their financial pyramid wider. This stage can involve different things for different people. It might mean investing into a small business that you're starting or investing in a friend's business. It could be buying very speculative individual stocks or aggressive specialty mutual funds.

Subjecting your money where the principal has a high degree of volatility and risk has potentially high returns, but your money could also be lost completely. It is appropriate that this stage fits at the top of the pyramid because if the money is lost, it won't be devastating to your overall financial plan.

My rule of thumb when deciding how much to risk in a business opportunity or other aggressive venture is one year's worth of net worth growth. Never invest more than this! In a worst case scenario, if you lost the entire amount of your investment, you have basically lost one year's worth of financial progress. While not fun, it is not financially devastating. People get into trouble and can't recover financially when they take a lifetime's worth of savings and gamble with it.

As an example, let's say that your net worth is $100,000, and conservatively projected a year from now, it will be $110,000. This growth could be from additional savings, reducing debts, and/or growth from your existing assets. In any event, the $10,000 projected growth is the amount that could be considered for a very speculative investment.

In the event that an opportunity has come along which requires more than this amount, do not be tempted to risk more. Consider lowering your investment, delaying the timing until your net worth has grown, or involving a financial partner.

In summary, no one has ever gotten into trouble financially by being too conservative for too long. Sure, there are some potential lost opportunity costs. But, you can get into a lot of financial trouble by being too aggressive with too much money. That's why the financial pyramid is such a useful tool to help organize and prioritize these decisions.

8

Frequently Asked Questions

Security and Confidence

1. *How much money should I have in emergency reserves?* As a general rule of thumb, you should have three to six months worth of bills easily available as emergency reserves. This doesn't necessarily have to be in a savings account. In fact, I currently have an approved line of credit against the equity of our home, and use that as my emergency reserve, minimizing my need to keep money in low yielding accounts.

2. *In which order and how should I go about paying off my debts?* Normally you'll want to pay off the highest after-tax interest loans to the lowest. It's important to consider the after-tax rate because certain loans are tax deductible while others are not. For example, the interest on your mortgage and student loan is usually deductible, but the interest on your car loan or credit card usually is not. Also take into consideration the total amount of the loan. If one low interest loan has a relatively low balance, but you would feel much better to get it out of your mind, then by all means pay it off!

3. *Which is the right type of life insurance and how much do I need?* Unfortunately, this is not an easy question to answer simply. Generally

you'll want to have at least five times your income and ideally up to fifteen times your income (human life value) in life insurance. A trusted insurance agent or financial planner can be a valuable resource in deciphering the many options, that meet your needs, and mesh with your overall financial plan.

4. *What are the most common financial mistakes people make?*

    a. Having their long-term money invested too conservatively.

    b. Having their short-term money invested too aggressively.

    c. Not planning for emergencies, or potential losses.

    d. Not planning for the future of their family business.

    e. Not taking the time to plan.

    f. Not seeking out the help of a qualified advisor.

5. *How can I appropriately measure my financial success?* Regularly updating your net worth statement will be an ideal way to gage your financial progress.

6. *When should I start saving and investing?* This is one of the few black and white answers in planning for your financial future. If you haven't started already, then the only correct response is *today!*

Capital Accumulation

1. *From a financial standpoint, is it better to buy or lease a car?* Like so many issues dealt with in this book, the answer here also depends on individual circumstances. When considering these two options, ask yourself the following questions:

- Do I need the security of low mileage and a warranty at all times?
- Do I plan to upgrade my vehicle every few years?
- Do I have the financial security to always make monthly car payments?
- Do I prefer the hassle of shopping for a new car periodically over that of having occasional breakdowns?

If you answered yes to these questions, then leasing may be the best option for you. However, if you would rather keep your car until the repair costs outweigh the cost of a monthly car payment, then buying a car outright makes more sense.

2. *What is a sales load on a mutual fund?* There are several fees that should be understood when making a mutual fund purchase:

- *Upfront sales load:* This cost takes on a greater significance the shorter time the fund is held. This is an up-front fee or commission to be used for compensation for the broker or financial planner or adviser. When doing your own research without the help of a third party, you may be more inclined to use a fund that does not have an up-front sales load. If you are using a financial advisor, then there is no problem with paying an up-front sales load if:

    a. You know how much the commission is (he/she should let you know).
    b. The amount you're paying is buying you worthwhile advice and saving you time.

- *Management fee:* This is the annual expense built into an investment. All funds have a management fee. Be sure you ask what the fee is and what that buys you in terms of service and value.

3. *What should I consider when buying a home?*

- Purchase a home valued at about double your gross annual income without a lot of stress on your budget. It is to your advantage to minimize the number of real estate transactions you engage in during your lifetime, because they involve substantial fees, commissions and transaction costs. Rather than getting a smaller "starter" home, requiring an upgrade in three to five years, try to stretch yourself a bit, especially when interest rates are lower and the housing market favorable.

- Be sure to have an attorney involved in the purchase. Because this is such an important financial commitment, a lawyer should look over the offer, closing statements, and other documents. The money you spend for an attorney will be well worth the peace of mind if brings.

- When financing, compare loan options as aggressively as you looked for your house. There are many differences among financial institutions in transaction fees, costs, and interest rates charged.

- In securing a loan, put down as small a down payment as the bank will allow and use a thirty-year mortgage. Use a fixed rate if you plan to be in the house seven years or longer. Use an adjustable rate if you plan to stay in the house less than seven years. Keep in mind if you have a 6 percent mortgage, the real cost to you would be approximately 4.3 percent, because you can deduct the interest. Assuming you can earn an after-tax rate of return of 4.4 percent or better, your net worth will grow faster by investing that money elsewhere.

• Try to avoid Private Mortgage Insurance with a combination of two loans, if possible. One loan is the traditional mortgage, and the other is held by the bank as a home equity line of credit at interest only.

• Other methods of preserving a good cash flow and keeping the up-front costs to a minimum include making an offer subject to the seller paying some of the closing costs, including appliances, etc in the offer. A good realtor and lawyer can be creative with this, depending upon the circumstances of the sale.

• Unless you use a buyer's broker, the real estate agent represents the *seller* in the transaction. They will work their hardest to find a place that you are satisfied with, but ultimately have a fiduciary responsibility to obtain the highest price they can for the seller.

4. *What's the best way to save for my child's college education?* There are many options available and doing some research will be necessary in order to find out which will work best for you. A 529 Plan is my favorite option that has tax advantages which varies according to state. To find out more, check www.savingforcollege.com.

General

1. *How do I make some tough decisions about my finances?* First of all, if a decision is hard to make, then either the timing isn't right, or you don't

have enough facts. So, I suggest to keep researching and asking questions until you feel more comfortable with the decision.

2. *Do you have any advice for couples?* I think that all couples should respect each other's opinions on a financial subject. If they are at odds, it may be because one person is thinking about the decision from the financial perspective and the other is looking at it from the emotional standpoint. Listen to each other and try to find the common ground. Also, consider establishing a dollar limit on decisions that must be made together and in agreement. For instance, if a financial purchase or decision is something which would cost $250 or more, then both people must agree on the decision.

9

Additional Resources

Glossary

Annuities, Fixed	An investment marketed by an insurance company that pays a guaranteed rate of return.
Annuity, Variable	An investment marketed by an insurance company with premiums mostly converted into separate accounts invested in stocks, bonds and money market accounts.
Assets	An investment or property that has value.
	Those assets that do not have a major loss of principal. These would include the most conservative assets in your portfolio like checking and savings accounts, money market funds, certificates of deposit, T-bills, EE savings bonds, whole life insurance cash values.
"Bear" market	A period of time in which securities are declining in price.

"Bull" market	A period of time in which securities are rising in price.
Capital	Money or other assets.
Certificate of Deposit	An account at a bank, savings and loan, and/or credit union which pays a fixed rate over a certain period of time.
CFP	A Certified Financial Planner is a person who advises others on achieving long-term financial goals, either for a fee or on commission basis. Ethics and professional standards are monitored by the CFP Board: www.cfp-board.org
ChFC	Chartered Financial Consultant—a degree earned through the American College.
Debt	Owing money
Diversification	Spreading your risk amongst various accounts to reduce volatility.
Dollar Cost Averaging	The buying of a fixed dollar amount of stock shares at regular intervals so that more shares are bought at low prices, fewer at high, resulting in an average cost that is lower than the

average price.

Inflation	A period of time marked by rising prices.
IRA	An Individual Retirement Account.
Liquidity	How easy is it to convert your investment into cash.
Money Market Mutual Fund	A pool of assets invested in bank CDs, T-Bills and commercial paper and considered the best emergency reserve account due to extreme safety and liquidity.
Portfolio	A listing of securities held by an investor or organization.
Principal	The current balance owed on a debt or the value of an account.
MSFS	Master of Financial Services. An advanced degree earned by the American College.
Mutual fund	A general term for an open-end investment company compromised of investments in basically any category.

Securities   Investments

Stock/share   A certificate representing ownership in a corporation that
                  usually sold to raise money to begin or expand a business.

T Bills   Treasury bill, a short-term federal obligation of the U.S
                  Treasury sold at a discount.

For Further Information:

The following is a very brief list of some of the resources for the individual interested in personal financial planning. To list all the helpful information available today would be a book in itself, so included here are some of the most popular and my personal favorites. The opinions and strategies expressed in the following sources should not be acted upon without first discussing them with a qualified investment, tax and/or legal advisor.

Newspapers

The Wall Street Journal is the most widely read business newspaper. It also has daily articles about investing and money matters.

Barron's is a weekly newspaper that reviews the stock markets. The Lipper Analytical Services mutual fund performance rating are included on a quarterly basis. There are also frequent articles on mutual fund investing

Investor's Business Daily is an excellent newspaper with a broad range of articles on finance, business and the economy.

New York Times and *USA Today* both have excellent business sections.

Magazines

Money magazine's December, January and February issues usually have articles on tax and investment planning.

Kiplinger's Personal Finance magazine's January issue focuses on financial planning (including tax planning) for the coming year. Mutual funds are reviewed in the September issue.

Smart Money offers articles on investing and financial planning.

Forbes is a bi-weekly investment magazine that looks at news from an investment point of view and has an annual mutual fund survey usually published in August.

Business Week focuses on current business news and contains articles on personal business, investing and financial planning.

Books

Golf is Not a Game of Perfect by Bob Rotella has nothing to do with financial planning. But....since I'm addicted to the great sport of golf and am always trying to improve, and see others improve, I recommend this book any time I get a chance. It provides some great ideas on the mental side of the game.

The New RetireMentality by Mitch Anthony is a great new book that identifies the issues facing everyone as they plan their future. This is especially helpful to those who are worried about what they will do during their retirement years.

There's No Place Like a Nursing Home by Karen Shoff is a must-read book for anyone who needs more education on long-term care for themselves or their loved ones.

The Ultimate Gift by Jim Stovall provides a very interesting story about wealth and the transfer of wealth to the next generation. I would suggest this book for anyone who wants to instill a sense of values and work ethic into their children, employees, etc.

Web sites

www.wallstreetcity.com has just about everything you need to know about stocks including free quotes, research and criteria-based charts matching your specifications.

www.investorama.com lists information of thousands of online financial sites.

www.quicken.com includes a wealth of personal finance information as well as calculators and interactive financial formulas.

www.bloomberg.com offers financial market reports.

www.sec.gov is the official site of the Securities and Exchange Commission.

www.savingforcollege.com discusses the multitude of state 529 college plans available and each of their advantages.

www.morningstar.com features a comprehensive review of mutual funds, and portfolio tracking.

www.savingsbonds.gov lists everything you need to know about US Savings Bonds.

www.irs.gov provides information on the publications and forms for most tax questions.

ABOUT THE AUTHOR

Certified Financial Planner Todd D. Bramson has been working in the field of financial planning for over 20 years and has been recognized as one of the 150 best financial advisors for doctors nationwide in the August 2000, and December 2002 issues of Medical Economics. An exceptional teacher, motivating author and speaker, he has been quoted in numerous financial publications and spent several years as the financial expert on the local NBC live 5 p.m. news broadcast. In June 2004 he spoke at the prestigious Million Dollar Round Table, a worldwide organization of the top 5 percent of all financial services professionals.

Bramson's belief that "if the trust is there, the miles don't matter" has earned him devoted clients not only in his hometown of Madison, Wisconsin, but in almost every state in the country. Along with all the advanced degrees expected of a trusted financial professional, he is committed to keeping abreast of all the developments in his field and to playing an active role in his community. Bramson conducts regular public seminars and is active in his church, the Breakfast Optimist Club, Evans Scholars Alumni Foundation, and Blackhawk Country Club.

NORTH STAR RESOURCE GROUP

North Star Resource Group is made up of:
North Star Consultants, Inc., CRI Securities, Inc., and
Marathon Advisors, Inc.

North Star Consultants, Inc.
Insurance Products & Services

CRI Securities, Inc. - *Registered Representative*
Securities & Investments
Member NASD/SIPC

Marathon Advisors, Inc. - *Investment Advisor*
Representative
Registered Investment Advisor

Securian Financial Services, Inc. - Registered
Representative
Variable Products & Securities
Member NASD/SIPC

CRI Securities, Inc. is affiliated with North Star Consultants, Inc.,
Marathon Advisors, Inc., and Securian Financial Services, Inc.
Securian Financial Services, Inc. operates under separate
ownership
from North Star Consultants, Inc. and Marathon Advisors, Inc.

Todd D. Bramson, CFP
North Star Resource Group
2945 Triverton Pike Drive #200
Madison, WI 53711
1-608-271-9100 ext.218
todd.bramson@northstarfinancial.com

Assets

Fixed:

Variable:

Personal and Other:

Total:

Liabilities:

Net Worth: Assets minus Liabilities_____

Budget

Notes

Notes

Notes

Notes

Notes

Management
Best Sellers

Other Best Sellers

- The Golf Course Locator for Business Professionals – Golf Courses Closest to Largest Companies, Law Firms, Cities & Airports, 180 Pages, $12.95

- Deal Teams - Roles and Motivations of Management Team Members, Venture Capitalists, Investment Bankers, Lawyers & More in Mergers, Acquisitions and Equity Investments - $27.95

- 10 Technologies Every Executive Should Know - Executive Summaries of the 10 Most Important Technologies Shaping the Economy - $17.95

- Software Agreements Line by Line - How to Understand & Change Software Licenses & Contracts to Fit Your Needs - $49.95

- Business Travel Bible – Must Have Phone Numbers, Business Resources & Maps, 240 Pages, $14.95

- Living Longer, Working Stronger – Simple Steps for Business Professionals to Capitalize on Better Health, 160 Pages, $14.95

- Business Grammar, Style & Usage – Rules for Articulate and Polished Business Writing and Speaking, 100 Pages, $14.95

- ExecRecs – Executive Recommendations For The Best Business Products & Services, 140 Pages, $14.95

- Executive Adventures – 50+ Exhilarating Out of the Office Escape Vacations, 100 Pages, $14.95

- The C-Level Test – Business IQ & Personality Test for Professionals of All Levels, 60 Pages, $17.95

- The Business Translator – Business Words, Phrases & Customs in Over 65 Languages, 540 Pages, $29.95

- Term Sheets & Valuations (CD-ROM - Customizable) - Includes an NDA, Due Diligence Checklist, and Term Sheet (From Above Book) in a Word Doc That can be Customized - $49.95